# Who Works at the Store?

Jay Krasinski



Infomax Readers

Rosen Classroom™

New York

Published in 2013 by The Rosen Publishing Group, Inc.
29 East 21st Street, New York, NY 10010



Book Design: Katelyn Londino

Photo Credits: Cover Andersen Ross/Iconica/Getty Images; p. 4 GM Visuals/Blend Images/Getty Images; pp. 5, 16 (neighborhood) Hisham Ibrahim/Photographer's Choice RF/Getty Images; pp. 6, 14 Tanya Constantine/Blend Images/Getty Images; p. 7 Wealan Pollard/OJO Images/Getty Images; p. 8 Andersen Ross/Digital Vision/Getty Images; pp. 9, 16 (candy) Suzanne Tucker/Shutterstock.com; p. 10 David Oliver/Taxi/Getty Images; p. 11 Piotr Sikora/Photonica/Getty Images; p. 12 Kzenon/Shutterstock.com; p. 13 Catalin Petolea/Shutterstock.com; p. 16 (grocery store) Jonathan Feinstein/Shutterstock.

ISBN: 978-1-4488-8956-3
6-pack ISBN: 978-1-4488-8957-0

Manufactured in the United States of America

CPSIA Compliance Information: Batch #WS12RC: For further information contact Rosen Publishing, New York, New York at 1-800-237-9932.

Word Count: 123

# Contents

My friends and I like to go shopping for many things.

There are many stores
in my neighborhood.

Who works at the toy store?

Mr. Jones works at the toy store.

What do I buy from Mr. Jones?

I buy a ball.

Who works at the candy store?

Miss Miller works at the candy store.

What does Matt buy from Miss Miller?

Matt buys candy.

Who works at the shoe store?

Mrs. Cook works at the shoe store.

What does Lisa buy from Mrs. Cook?

Lisa buys shoes for school.

Who works at the grocery store?

Mr. Taylor works at the grocery store.

What does John buy from Mr. Taylor?

John buys apples.

Shopping is fun!

What are your favorite things to buy?

# My Shopping Trip

| Where Do We Go? | Who Works There? | What Do We Buy There? |
| --- | --- | --- |
| toy store | Mr. Jones | ball |
| candy store | Miss Miller | candy |
| shoe store | Mrs. Cook | shoes for school |
| grocery store | Mr. Taylor | apples |

# Words to Know

candy

grocery store

neighborhood

# Index